THE MOST REQUESTED
Classic Rock Songs

Cherry Lane Music Company
Director of Publications/Project Editor: Mark Phillips

ISBN 978-1-60378-327-9

CONTENTS

Africa

Words and Music by
David Paich and Jeff Porcaro

I hear the drums

ech-o-in' to-night.___ She hears on-ly whis-pers of some

qui-et con-ver-sa - tion.

She's com-ing in, twelve thir-ty flight.___ as
The wild dogs cry out in the night,___

Moon-lit wings___ re-flect the stars___ that guide me toward sal-y-
they grow rest-less, long-ing for___ some sol-i-tar-y

There's noth-ing that a hun-dred men _ or more _ could ev - er do. _

I bless the rains _ down in Af -

ri - ca. _ Gon - na take some time _

_ to do _ the things we nev - er had. _

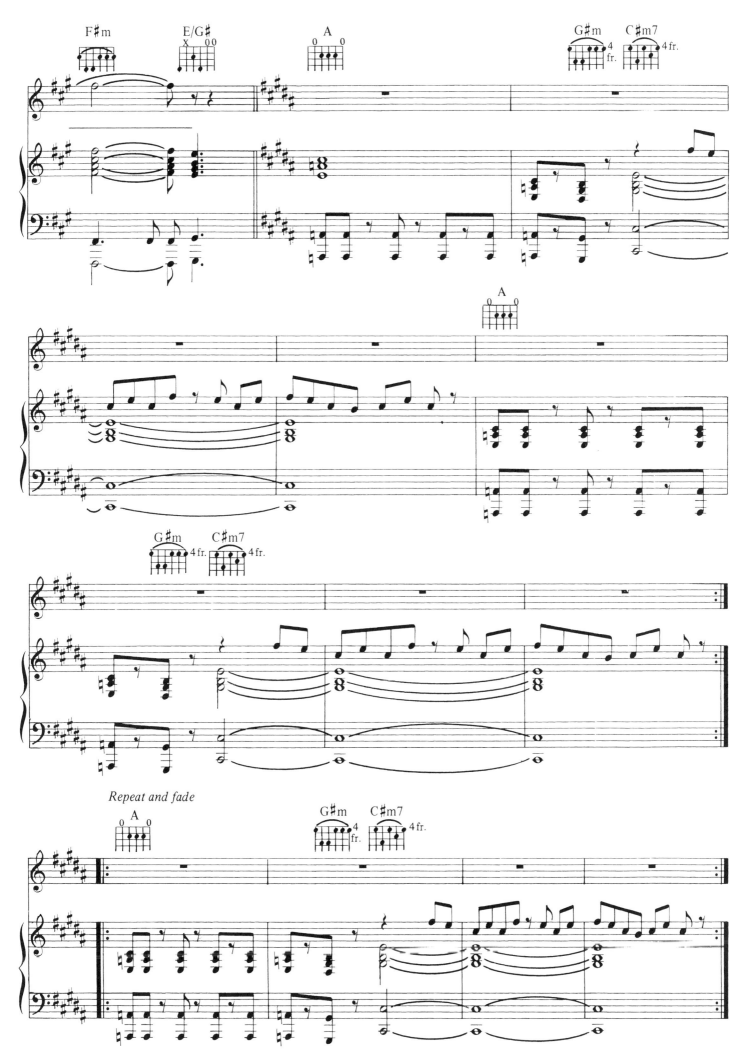

9

Baby Hold On

Words and Music by
Eddie Money and James Douglas Lyon

D.S. al Coda I

CODA I

D.S. al Coda II

CODA II

Bang a Gong

(Get It On)

Words and Music by
Marc Bolan

Verse 1-3: To next strain
Verse 4: Repeat and Fade

16

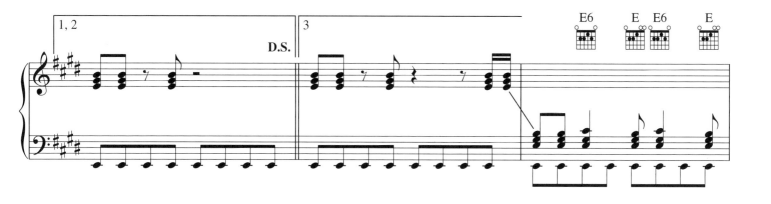

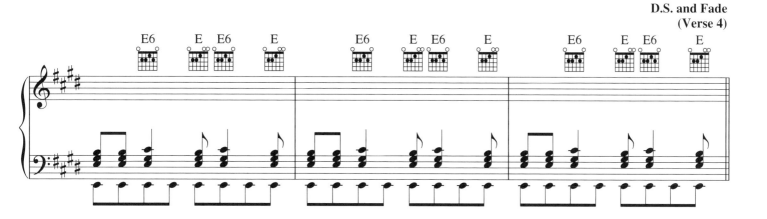

Additional Lyrics

2. You're built like a car
   You've got a hub cap diamond star halo
   You're built like a car, oh yeah.
   You're an untamed youth that's the truth
   With your cloak full of eagles
   You're dirty sweet and you're my girl.
   Chorus

3. You're windy and wild
   You've got the blues in your shoes and your stockings
   You're windy and wild, oh yeah.
   You're built like a car
   You've got a hub cap diamond star halo
   You're dirty sweet and you're my girl.
   Chorus

4. You're dirty and sweet
   Clad in black, don't look back and I love you.
   You're dirty and sweet, oh yeah.
   You dance when you walk
   So let's dance, take a chance, understand me
   You're dirty sweet and you're my girl.
   Chorus and Fade

Bad Moon Rising

Words and Music by
John Fogerty

I see bad ___ times to - day.
I hear the voice of rage and ruin. ___
One eye is tak - en for an eye. ___

Don't go a - round to - night, ___ well, it's bound to take ___ your life. ___

To Coda

There's a bad ___ moon on the rise. ___

1, 2   3

D.S. al Coda

CODA

Cold As Ice

Words and Music by
Mick Jones and Lou Gramm

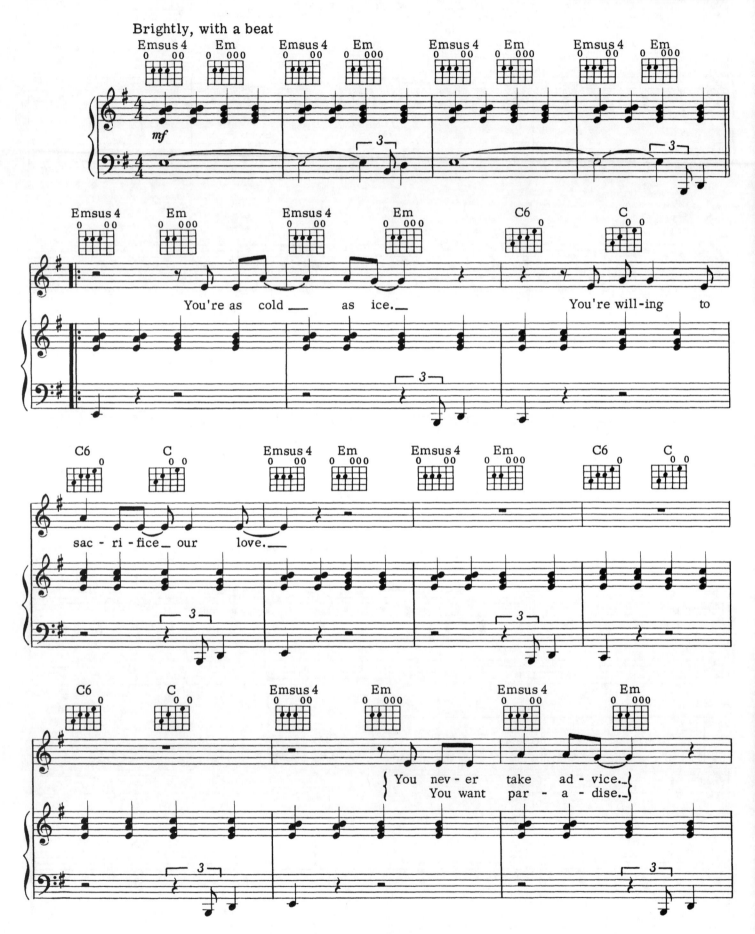

some-day you'll pay.

Cold   as

Dear Mr. Fantasy

Words and Music by
James Capaldi, Chris Wood
and Steve Winwood

You are the one ___ who ___ can make us all ___ laugh ___ but do-ing that ___ you break out in

tears. _____ Please don't be sad, ___ if it ___ was a

straight mind you had, _____ we would-n't have known you all ___ these years. ___

Ooh, _____ aah, ooh, _____

To Coda ⊕

ahh,   ooh, _____ ahh,

ooh,   ahh,   ahh.

Dear Mis - ter Fan - ta - sy play us a tune, _____ some-thing _ to make _ us all _ hap -

py. _____   Do an - y - thing, take _ us   out of this _ gloom. _ Sing a song, _

26

play gui-tar, __ make it snap - py, _____ yeah _ yeah. *Ad lib. instrumental solo*

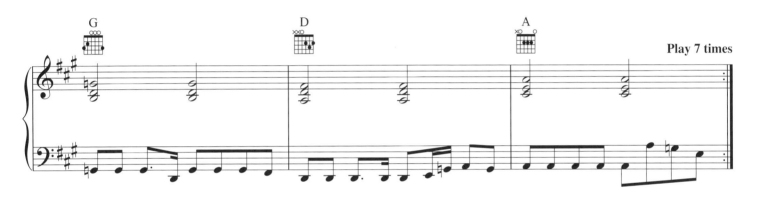

Play 7 times

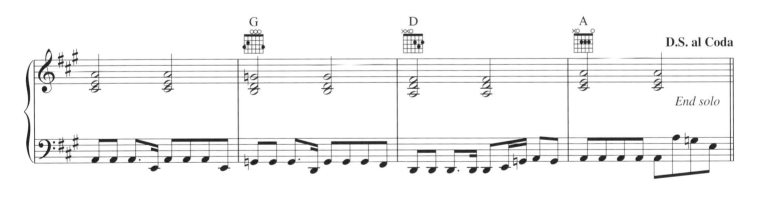

D.S. al Coda

End solo

CODA

Ad lib. instrumental solo

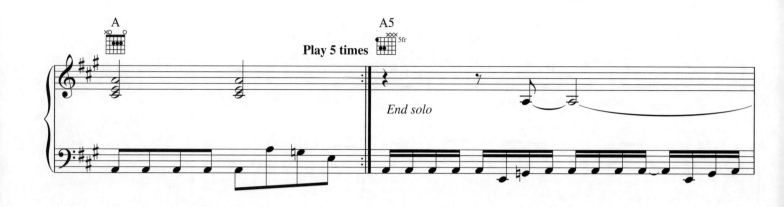

Diamond Girl

Words and Music by
James Seals and Dash Crofts

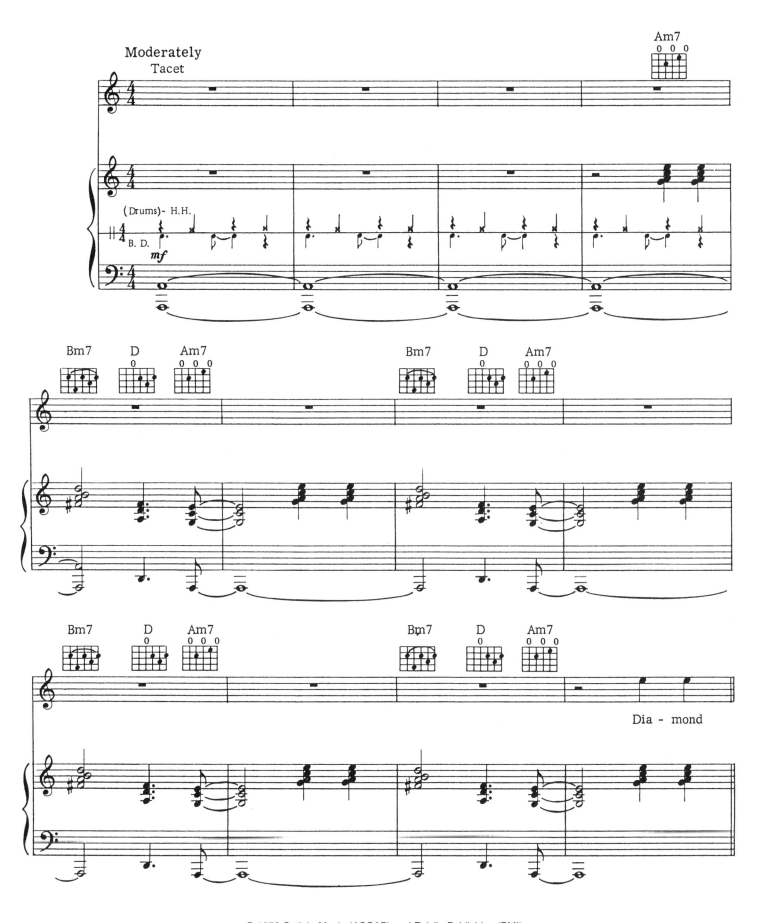

girl,   you sure do___ shine,   glad I___

found you,   glad you're mine.   Oh, my___ love,___

Shuffle rhythm (♩♩ = ♩³♩)

you're like a pre - cious stone,

part of earth_____   where heav-en has rained___

you ___ that I am? _____ a - woah, ___

woah, oh, ___ oh. _____

Dia - mond girl, roam - in' wild,

32

such a rare thing, ra-di-ant child.

Shuffle rhythm (♪♪ = ♪ ♪)

I could nev-er find _____ an-oth-er one like_

_ you, _____ part of me _____

is deep down in - side ___ you. ___ Can't you feel_

Do You Feel Like We Do

Words and Music by
Peter Frampton, John Siomos,
Rick Wills and Mick Gallagher

Don't Stop Believin'

Words and Music by
Steve Perry, Neal Schon
and Jonathan Cain

Just a small - town girl, _____
Just a cit - y boy, _____

A sing - er in a smok - y room. ____

The smell of wine and cheap per - fume. ____ For a smile _ they can

share the night. It goes on and on ___ and on ___ and on. ___

Stran - gers ___ wait - ing ___ up and down the
Street - light ___ peo - ple, ___ liv - ing just to

boul - e - vard, ___ their shad - ows ___ search - ing ___ in the night. ___
find e - mo - tion, hid - ing ___

some - where ___ in the night. ___

D.S. (with repeat) al Coda

Dreams

Words and Music by
Stevie Nicks

It's on - ly right ____
It's on - ly me ____

___ that you _ should play the way _ you feel ____ it. But
___ who wants _ to wrap a - round _ your dreams. _ And

lis - ten care - ful - ly _____ to the sound _____ of your lone-
have you an - y dreams _ you'd like to sell? ____ Dreams of lone-

li - ness, like a heart - beat, drives you mad, _____ in the still-
li - ness, like a heart - beat, drives you mad, _____ in the still-

49

Play-ers on-ly love ___ you when they're play-ing. ___ Say, wom-en, they will come ___ and they will go. ___ When the rain ___ wash-es ___ you clean, you'll know. ___

To Coda ⊕

The End of the Innocence

Words and Music by
Bruce Hornsby and Don Henley

O

Coda

Just lay your head __ back __ on __ the ground __ and let your hair __ fall all __ a - round __ me. __ Of - fer up __ your best __

58

Feelin' Alright

Words and Music by
Dave Mason

Im - pris - oned by the way __ it could have been, _____
that when I think of you __ I start my - self to cry. _____
But that was then, and now __ you know it's to - day. _____

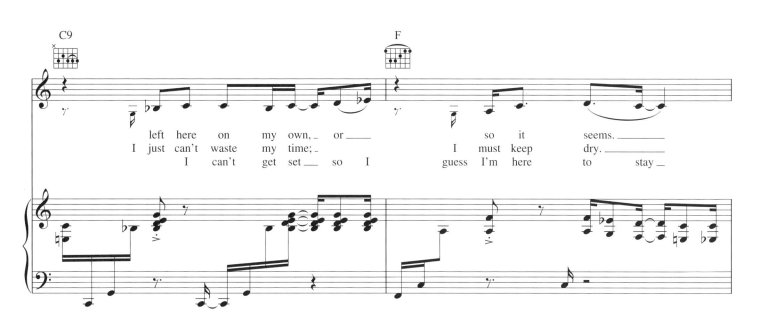

I left here on my own, __ or _____ so it seems. _____
I just can't waste my time; _ I must keep dry. _____
I can't get set __ so I guess I'm here to stay __

I got to leave be - fore __ I _____ start to __ scream,
Got - ta stop be - liev - in' in all your __ lies,
un - til some - one comes a - long __ and _____ takes my __ place

'cause ___ some-one's locked the door and ___ took the key. ___
'cause ___ there's too much to do be ___ fore I die. ___
with a dif-f'rent name, ___ woh, and a dif-f'rent face. ___

You're feel-in'

Chorus

al - right?   (Oh,   oh.)   I'm   not   feel - in' too good ___

___ my - self.   (Oh,   oh.)

Yes, ___ sir.
Oh, ___ no.
Mm. _____

You feel - in'

al - right?   (Oh,   oh.)

1.3. I'm   not   feel - in' that good ___
2. I'm   not   feel - in' too good, ___

62

Forever Young

Words and Music by
Rod Stewart, Kevin Savigar,
Jim Cregan and Bob Dylan

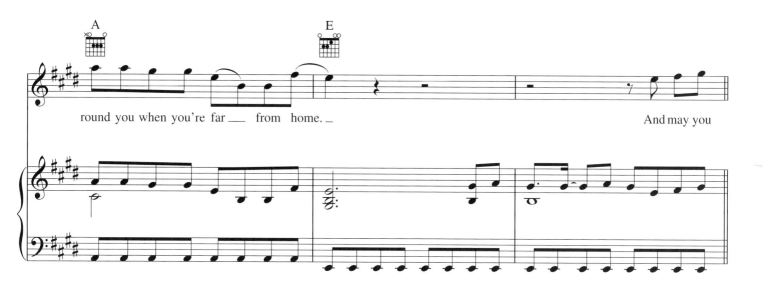

round you when you're far __ from home. __ And may you

grow __ to be proud, __ dig - ni - fied __ and true. __
for - tune be with you, may your guid - ing light __ be strong, _
fi - n'lly fly a - way, I'll be hop - ing that I served __ you well. __

—— And do un - to oth - ers as
—— build a stair-way to heav-en with a
—— For all the wis - dom of a life - time,

you'd have done to you. _____
prince or a vag - a - bond. _____
no one can ev - er tell. _____

Be cou - ra - geous and _____ be brave. _____
And may you nev - er love _____ in vain.
But what - ev - er road _____ you choose, _____

And in my heart you'll al - ways stay _____
And in my heart you will _____ re - main _____
I'm right be - hind you, win _____ or lose, _____

for - ev - er young. (For - ev - er

young) For - ev - er young. (For - ev - er

1

young) ___ May good

2, 3

young) ___

For - ev - er

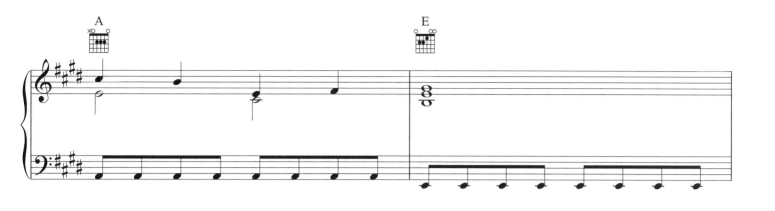

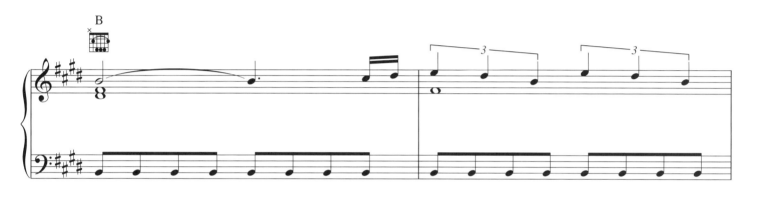

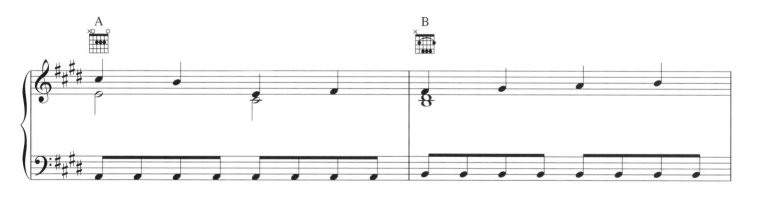

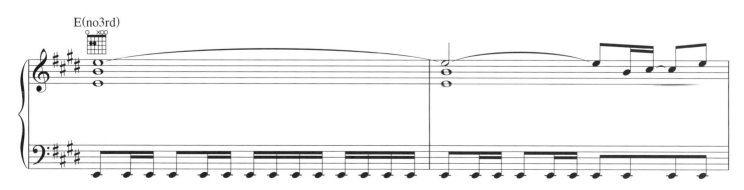

Hello, It's Me

Words and Music by
Todd Rundgren

you as mine. ___
all the way through. ___

It's im-por-tant to me _____ that you know you are free, ___

_____ 'cause I nev - er want to make you change ___ for

me.

Think of me,

A Horse with No Name

Words and Music by
Dewey Bunnell

been thru the des - ert on a horse with no name. _ It felt

good to be out ___ of the rain. _____ In the

des - ert _____ you can re - mem - ber your name _ 'cause there

ain't no one for to give you no pain. _ La la la

To Coda ⊕

I Can See for Miles

Words and Music by
Peter Townshend

I know you've de-ceived me. Now here's a sur-prise.

I know that you have 'cause there's mag-ic in ___ my eyes. I can see for

82

I Won't Back Down

Words and Music by
Tom Petty and Jeff Lynne

And I won't ___ back down. ___ Hey ___

___ ba - by, there ain't no eas - y way out. ___

Hey, ___ I ___ will

stand my ground, ___ and I won't back down. ___ Well, I

CODA

Hey _____ ba - by,

there ain't no eas - y way out. ____ Hey, _____ I ____ will stand my ground, ____ and I won't back down. ____ No I won't back down. ____

I've Seen All Good People
Your Move

Words and Music by
Jon Anderson and Chris Squire

to use. Move me on __ to an - y black square,

use me an - y time __ you want, Just re - mem - ber that __

__ the gold __ 'sfor us all to cap - ture all we want __

an - y - where, __ Yea, __ yea __

91

All Good People

F G C
- is - fied I'm on my way. I've seen all good peo -
poco dim.
mp
B♭ A♭ 4fr E♭ 3fr
- ple turn their heads each day so sat - is fied I'm on
F B♭ A♭ 4fr
my way. I've seen all good peo - ple turn their heads
poco dim.
p
G♭ D♭ E♭ 3fr
each day so sat - is - fied I'm on my way.
dim.

In the Air Tonight

Words and Music by
Phil Collins

100

Well, I've been wait-ing for this mo ment for all my life, _____ oh Lord. _____

_____ oh Lord. _____

Well, I re - mem - ber, I re -

mem-ber, don't wor - ry. How could I _____ ev - er for - get? It's the

first time, ___ the last time ___ we ev - er met.

But I _____ know the rea - son ___ why ___ you keep the si - lence up.

No, you don't fool me. The hurt does - n't show, but the

pain ___ still grows. _____ It's no stran - ger to you ___ or me.

D.S. and Fade

Keep On Loving You

Words and Music by
Kevin Cronin

but you nev-er bled. In-stead you laid still in the grass ___ all coiled up and hiss-

-in'. ___ And though I know all a-

Instrumental

bout those men, ___ still I don't re-mem-ber. ___

'Cause it was us, ba-by, way be-fore them, ___ and we're still to-geth-er. ___

Lay Down Sally

Words and Music by
Eric Clapton, Marcy Levy
and George Terry

Bright beat

There is noth - ing that __ is wrong __ in want - ing you __ to stay __
sun ain't near - ly on __ the rise, __ and we still got __ the moon __
long to see __ the morn - ing light __ col - or - ing your face __

__ here __ with me.
__ and stars __ a - bove.
__ so dream - i - ly.

I
So

109

Layla

Words and Music by
Eric Clapton and Jim Gordon

Recorded a whole step lower.

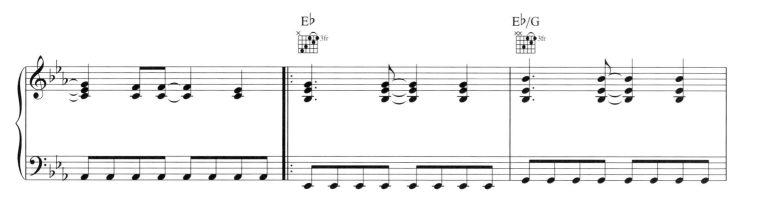

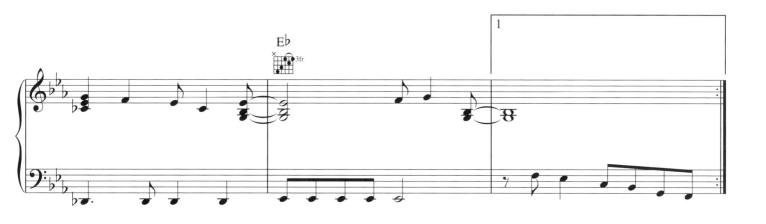

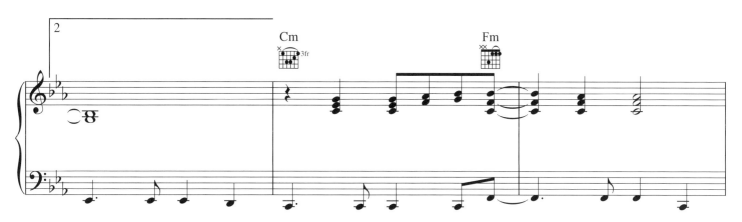

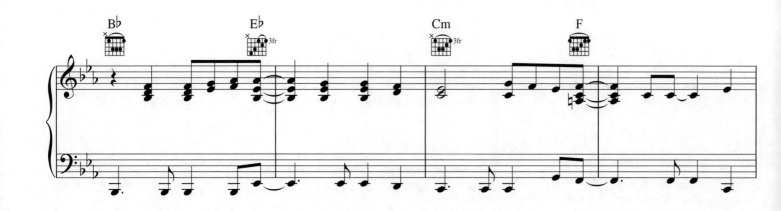

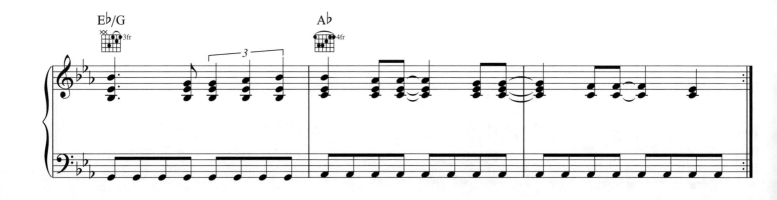

Freely

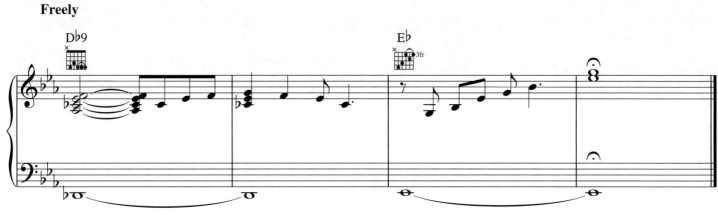

Let It Be

Words and Music by
John Lennon and Paul McCartney

let it be. _____ There will be ____ an an - swer; let it be. ____

Let it be, ____ let it be, ____ let it be, ____

let it be. ____

Whis - per words ___ of wis - dom; let it be. ____
There will be ____ an an - swer; let it be. ____

Let It Ride

Words and Music by
Randy Bachman and Charles Turner

Good - bye, _____ hard life, _____

don't cry. _____ Would you let it ride? _____

You can't see the morn - in', but I can see the light. _
Babe, my life is not _ com - plete; I nev - er see you smile. _

Ride, ride, ride, let it ride. _
Ride, ride, ride, let it ride. _

While you've been out run - nin', I've _ been wait - in' half the night. _
Ba - by, you want the for - giv - in' kind _ and that's just not my style. _
I've been do - in' things worth - while _ and you've been book - in' time. _

Ride, ride, ride, let it ride. ___ And
would you cry ___ if I told you that _ I lied ___ and would you
say good-bye or would you let it ride? ___ And
would you cry ___ if I told you that _ I lied, ___ and would you

say good - bye   or would you let it ride?____

D.S. al Coda

Coda

F#m

Would you let it ride?_

Would you let it ride?_

Would you let it ride?_

124

Would you let it ride?_

Would you let it ride?_

Would you let it ride?_

Would you let it ride?_

D   A   E   F#m

Bm9   F#m7

Repeat and fade

126

The Letter

Words and Music by
Wayne Carson Thompson

Moderately, with a double-time feel

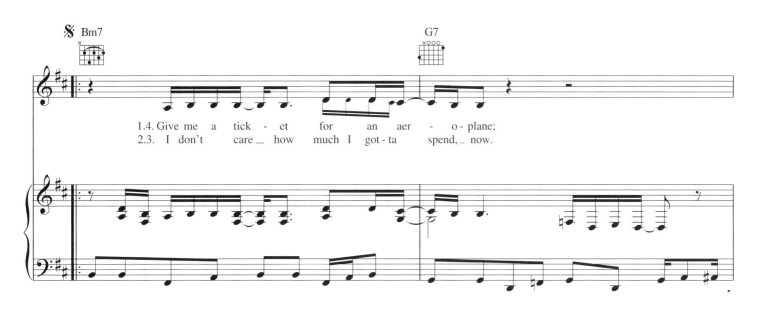

1.4. Give me a tick - et for an aer - o - plane;
2.3. I don't care __ how much I got - ta spend, __ now.

I ain't __ got time _____ to take no fast train.
Woh, I _____ will find _____ my way back home a - gain.

*Recorded a half step lower.

128

me no more.

D   A   G   D

Listen to me, mister, can't you see I'm ready for my

A

baby once more?

To Coda I

F#7

D.S. (take 2nd ending) al Coda I

An-y-way...

Coda I   F#7

D.S. al Coda II

An-y-way...

Coda II   Bm   D   E   D   E   D

My

129

Lido Shuffle

Words and Music by
Boz Scaggs and David Paich

Next ___ stop Chi - town, Li -
He be mak - in' like a bee - line

do put the mon - ey down and let ___ it roll. ___
head - in' for the bor - der line, go - in' for broke ___

He said, "One more ___ job ___ ought to get it,
say - in', "One more ___ hit ___ ought to do it,

one last ___ shot ___ 'fore we quit it,
this joint ___ ain't ___ noth - in' to it,

one for the road."
one more for the road."

Li - do, oh,

he's for the mon - ey, he's

for the show, Li - do's a - wait - in' for the go.

Life in the Fast Lane

Words and Music by Don Henley,
Glenn Frey and Joe Walsh

She held him up, and he held her for ran - som in the heart_
all the right peo - ple; they took all the right pills._____ They threw

_____ of the cold, cold_ cit - y. He had a
out - ra - geous par-ties; they paid heav - en - ly bills. There were

nas - ty rep - u - ta - tion as a cru - el dude._ They
lines on the mir - ror, lines on her face. She pre -

Life in the fast_ lane sure-ly make_ you lose_ your mind._

Life in the fast_ lane, mm._

Are you with me so far?

Life in the fast_ lane; ev-'ry-thing_ all the time._

To Coda

Life in the fast lane, uh huh.

Load-ed and burn-in', blind-ed by thirst, they

did-n't see the stop sign; took a turn for the worse. She said,

"Lis-ten, ba-by. You can hear the en-gine ring. We've been

140

up and down this high-way; have-n't seen a god-dam thing." He said,

"Call the doc-tor. I think I'm gon-na crash." The

doc-tor say he's com-in', but you got-ta pay in cash. And we're

rush-in' down that free-way; messed a-round and got lost.

Listen to the Music

Words and Music by
Tom Johnston

143

oh, lis-ten to the mu-sic,_ oh,_ oh, lis-ten to the

mu-sic_ all the time._

Like a la-zy flow-ing riv-er_ sur-round-ing cas-tles in the sky._

The Logical Song

Words and Music by
Rick Davies and Roger Hodgson

Moderate Rock

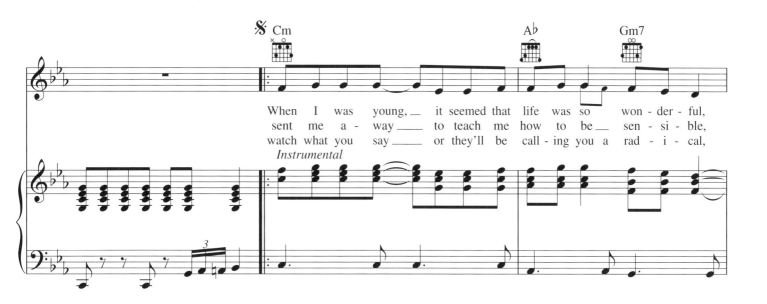

When I was young, __ it seemed that life was so won-der-ful,
sent me a-way __ to teach me how to be __ sen-si-ble,
watch what you say __ or they'll be call-ing you a rad-i-cal,

Instrumental

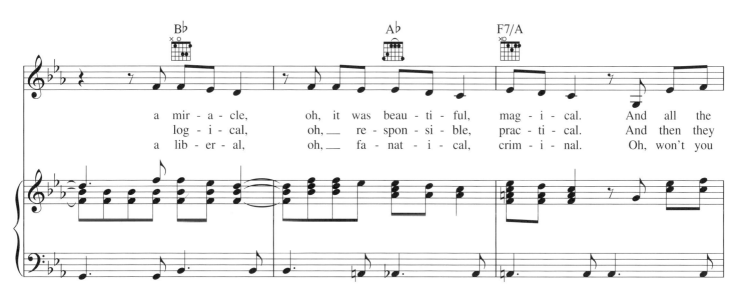

a mir-a-cle, oh, it was beau-ti-ful, mag-i-cal. And all the
log-i-cal, oh, __ re-spon-si-ble, prac-ti-cal. And then they
a lib-er-al, oh, __ fa-nat-i-cal, crim-i-nal. Oh, won't you

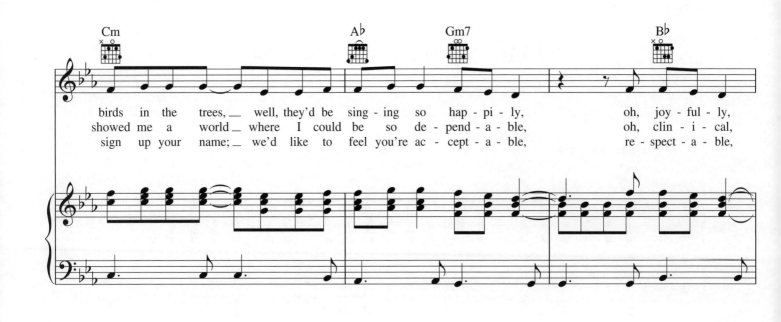

birds in the trees, __ well, they'd be sing - ing so hap - pi - ly,   oh, joy - ful - ly,
showed me a world __ where I could be so de - pend - a - ble,   oh, clin - i - cal,
sign up your name; __ we'd like to feel you're ac - cept - a - ble,   re - spect - a - ble,

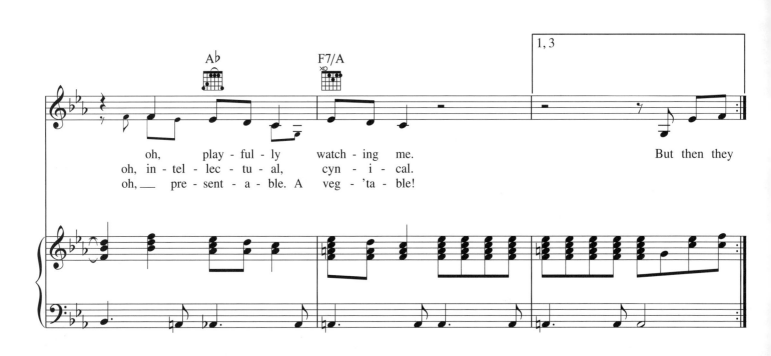

oh, play - ful - ly   watch - ing me.
oh, in - tel - lec - tu - al,   cyn - i - cal.
oh, __ pre - sent - a - ble. A veg - 'ta - ble!

But then they

There are times __)
Instrumental ends But at night, __)   when all __ the world's __ a - sleep, __

148

149

150

151

Magic Carpet Ride

Words and Music by
John Kay and Rushton Moreve

Heavy Metal Rock

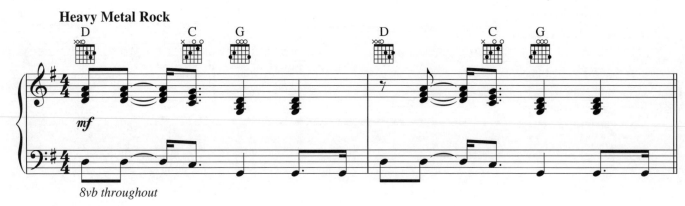

8vb throughout

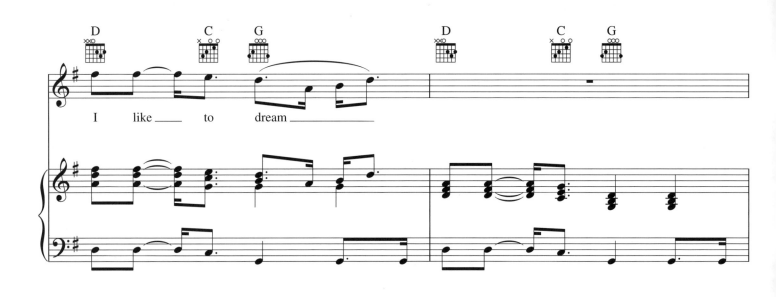

I like ___ to dream ___

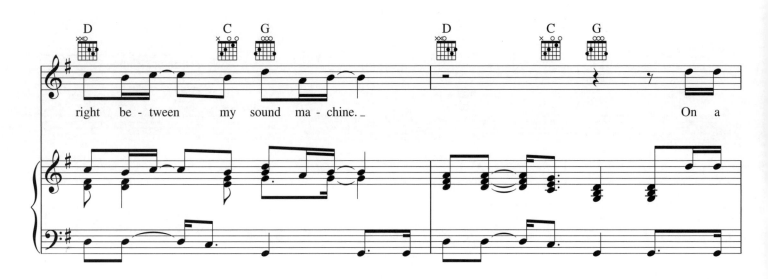

right be-tween my sound ma-chine. ___   On a

cloud of sound _ I drift in the night, _ an-y place it goes _ is right;

goes far, flies near, to the stars a-way _ from here. Well,

you _ don't know what we _ can find. Oh,

why don't you come with me, _ lit-tle girl, on a mag-ic car-pet ride. Well,

you ___ don't know what we can see.

Why don't you tell your dreams to me, fan - ta - sy ___ will set you free.

Close your eyes, girl, look in - side, girl, let the sound take you a-

To Coda ⊕

G(no3)

way.   Last

night I owned_ A - lad - din's lamp_ and so I wished that I could stay.

Be - fore the thing could an - swer me, some - one came and took the lamp a - way.

D.S. al Coda

I looked a - round, a lous - y can - dle is all I found. Well,

CODA G(no3)

way.

Maybe I'm Amazed

Words and Music by
Paul McCartney

1. Ba - by, I'm a - mazed at the way you love me all the time,
2. *Instrumental*
3. May - be I'm a - mazed at the way you're with me all the time,
4. *Instrumental*

and may - be I'm a - fraid of the way I love you.

and may - be I'm a - fraid of the way I need you.

157

Ba - by, I'm a man, and may - be you're the on - ly wom - an who could ev - er help me.

Ba - by, won't you help me to un - der - stand? Ooh.

3

D.S. al Coda

CODA

Repeat and Fade

Optional Ending

Minute by Minute

Words and Music by
Michael McDonald and Lester Abrams

F13sus4   F13

wor - ry.   I know where I stand.____   I don't need____ this
hab - it of liv - in' on the run.____   Take it all____ for

Am7/G   F/G

love.____   I don't need your hand.____   I know I could
grant - ed like you're the on - ly one.____   Liv - in' on my

F13sus4   F13

turn,   blink, and you'd be gone.   Then I must be____ pre -
own,   some - how that sounds nice.   You think I'm____ your

Am7/G   F/G

pared____ an - y time to car - ry on.____   But____
fool.____   Well, you may just be right.____

Money

Words and Music by
Roger Waters

Mon - ey, ya get a -
Mon - ey, you get
Mon - ey, it's a

way. Ya get a good job with more pay, and you're O -
back. I'm all right, Jack. Keep your hands off my __
crime. Share it fair - ly, but don't take a slice of

- K.

_____ stack.

my _____ pie.

Mon - ey,   it's   a

Mon - ey,   it's   a

Mon - ey,   so they

gas.

hit.

say,

Grab that cash with both hands and make ___

But don't give me that do - good - y good bull -

is the root of all e - vil to -

F♯m

___ a stash.

- shit.

- day.

New car, cav - i - ar, four - star day - dream.

I'm in the high fi - del - i - ty, first - class trav - 'ling

But if you ask for ___ a raise, it's no sur -

Think I'll buy me a foot - ball _____ team.
set, and I think I need a Lear _ jet.

prise that they're giv - ing none a - way. _

Repeat and Fade

166

Nights in White Satin

Words and Music by
Justin Hayward

yes, I __ love you. _____ Oh, _____ how I

love __ you. _____

love __ you. _____ Oh, __ how I love

you. _____

No Matter What

Written by
Peter Ham

say, noth-ing to see, ___ noth-ing to do. ___

If you would give me all, ___ as

I would give ___ it to ___ you, noth-ing would be, ___ noth-ing would

be, ___ noth-ing would be. _____

No mat-ter where you
No mat-ter what you

go, ____ there ____ will al - ways be a place. ____

are, ____ I ____ will al - ways be with you. ____

Can't you see it in my face, girl? ____

Does - n't mat - ter what you do, girl. ____

Ooh, ____ girl, ____ want

you. ____

Guitar solo

To Coda

D.S. al Coda

CODA

you. ___ Ooh, girl, ___

you, ___ girl, ___ want you. ___

Ooh, girl, ___ you, ___ girl, ___ want you. ___

174

November Rain

Words and Music by
W. Axl Rose

* Recorded a half step lower

When I look in - to — your eyes, I can see a love — re-strained. —

But dar - lin', when — I hold —

— you, don't you know I feel the same?

ken heart,— would-n't time— be out— to charm— you? Woh.——

And when your fears___ sub-side___

___ and shad-ows still___ re-main,

I know that you___ can love me when there's no one left to blame.___

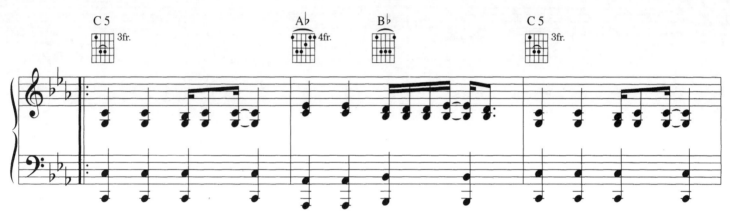

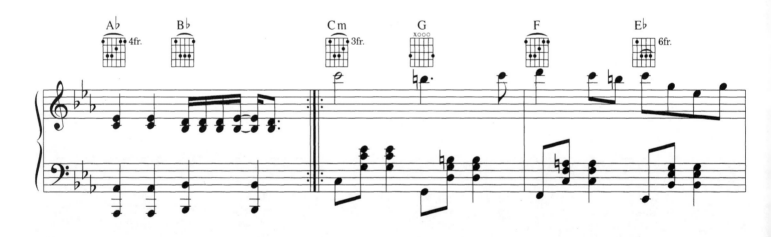

Old Time Rock & Roll

Words and Music by
George Jackson and Thomas E. Jones III

Moderate Rock 'n' Roll beat

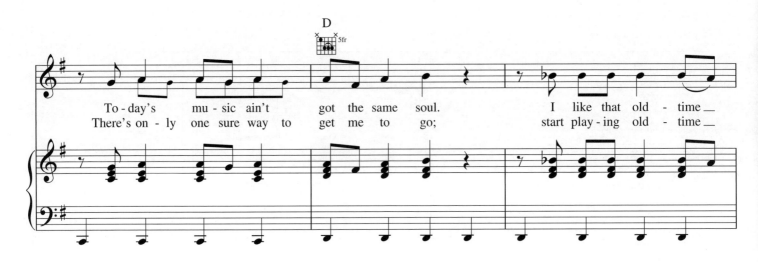

soothes my soul. __ I rem - i - nise a - bout the days of old __

with that old - time rock 'n' roll. __

1. *Guitar solo ad lib.*
2. *Saxophone solo ad lib.*

188

189

Only the Good Die Young

Words and Music by
Billy Joel

Send up a sig - nal, I'll throw you a line ___ that stained glass cur - tain you're
Some say it's bet - ter but I say it ain't ___ I'd rath - er laugh with the sin - ners than

hid - ing be - hind ___ nev - er lets in the sun ___ Dar - lin',
cry with the saints ___ The sin - ners are much more fun ___ You know that

on - ly the good ___ die young ___ Whoa ___
on - ly the good ___ die young ___ That's what I say

On - ly the good ___ die young ___ On - ly the
On - ly the good ___ die young ___ On - ly the

good die young
good die young _____ (Instrumental)

You got a nice white dress and a

par - ty on your con - fir - ma - tion _____

You've got a

brand new soul _____

and a cross of gold _____

_____ (End instrumental)

But Vir - gin - ia they did - n't give you quite e - nough in - for - ma -
Said your moth - er told you all that I could give you was a rep - u - ta -

194

196

Open Arms

Words and Music by
Steve Perry and Jonathan Cain

Our House

Words and Music by
Graham Nash

Moderately slow

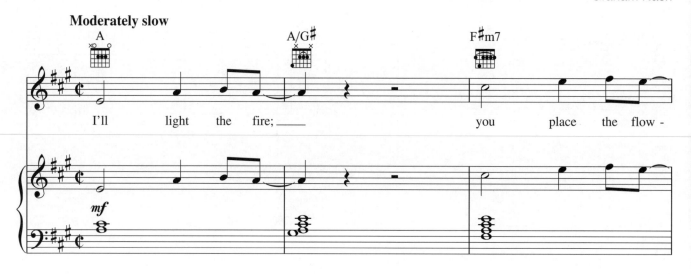

I'll light the fire; _____ you place the flow-

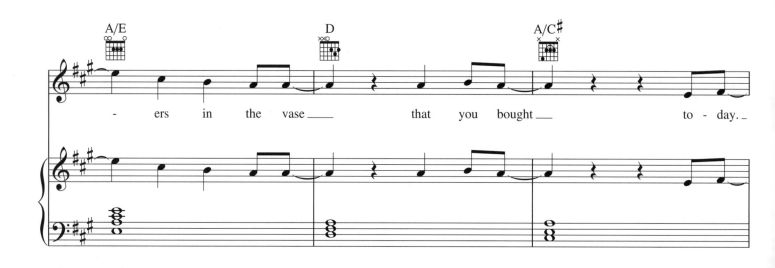

-ers in the vase _____ that you bought _____ to - day. _

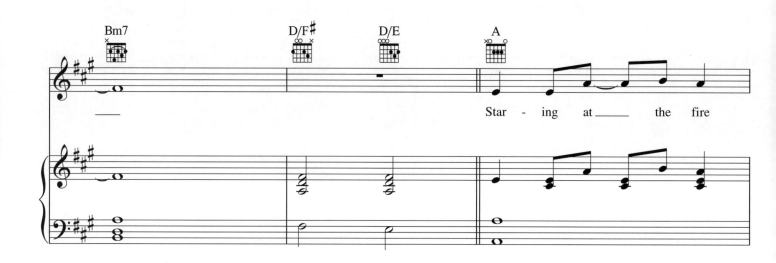

Star - ing at _____ the fire

for hours _____ and hours _____ while I

lis - ten to you play your

love songs all night long for

me, _____ on - ly for ___ me. ___

Come to me now ___ and rest ___ your head ___ for just ___
(Come to me now.) ___

___ five min - utes; ev - 'ry - thing is

done.

Such a co - zy room. ___

F#m7   A/E

(Such a co - zy room.) ___ The win - dows are il - lu - mi - nat - ed

D   A/C#   Bm7   D/C#

by   the   eve - ning   sun - shine

D/E   D/C#   Bm7   D/C#   D/E   D/C#

through them: Fi - ery gems for

A   A/G#   F#m7

you, _____ on - ly for ___ you. ___

la   la   la   la   la   la   la   la   la _____ la   la   la.

Our   house   is a   ver - y, ver - y, ver - y fine
                                                              (ver - y, ver - y,

house,   with two cats in the yard. ____   Life
ver - y fine house)

used to be ___ so   hard; _____   now ev - 'ry - thing ___ is eas -

Peace of Mind

Words and Music by
Tom Scholz

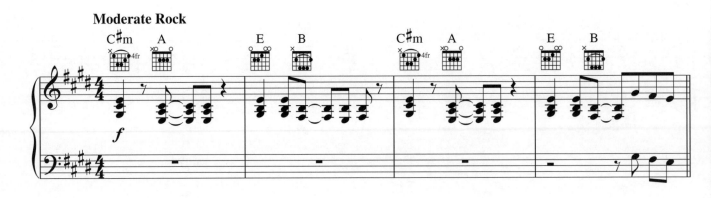

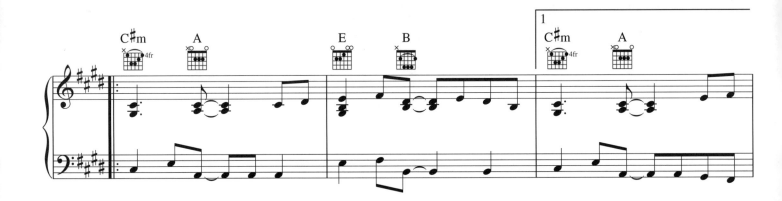

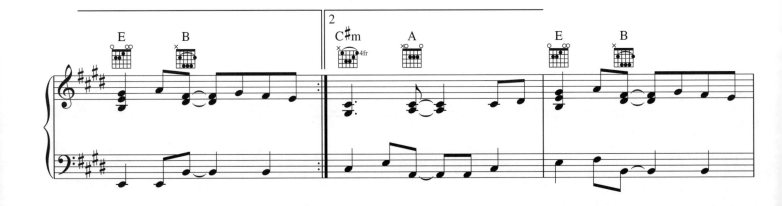

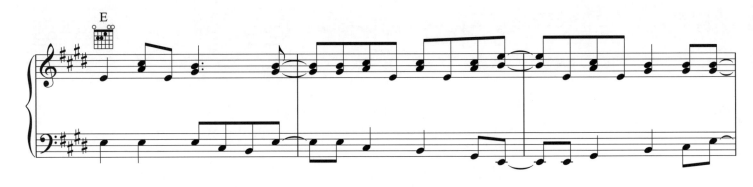

Now, if you're feel-in' kind-a low 'bout the dues you've been pay-in',
climb-in' to the top of the com-pa-ny lad-der,
bod-y's got ad-vice they just keep on giv-in',

fu-ture's com-in' much too ___ slow. ___ And you wan-na run but some-how you just
hope it does-n't take too ___ long. ___ Can't you see there'll come a day when
does-n't mean too much to me. ___ Lots of peo-ple have to make be-

keep on stay-in', can't de-cide on which way to go. ___ Whoa. ___
it won't mat-ter, come a day when you'll be gone. ___
lieve they're liv-in'; can't de-cide who they should be. ___

Yeah, yeah, yeah.
Whoa. _____
Whoa. _____

I un-der-stand __ a-bout in-de - ci - sion, __ but

I don't care __ if I get be - hind. __ Peo - ple liv - in' in

com - pe - ti - tion; all I want ___ is to have my peace ___ of ___

Yeah,   yeah, — yeah,   yeah. _____

D.S. al Coda
(take 2nd ending)

Now, ev -'ry -

Look a - head.

rit.   *a tempo*

Repeat and Fade

Pick Up the Pieces

Words and Music by
James Hamish Stuart, Alan Gorrie,
Roger Ball, Robbie McIntosh,
Owen McIntyre and Malcolm Duncan

pick up the piec - es.

Bb7sus

Sax solo

220

Fm7

Pick up the piec - es,

pick up the piec - es.

Pick up the

Rainy Day Women # 12 & 35

Words and Music by
Bob Dylan

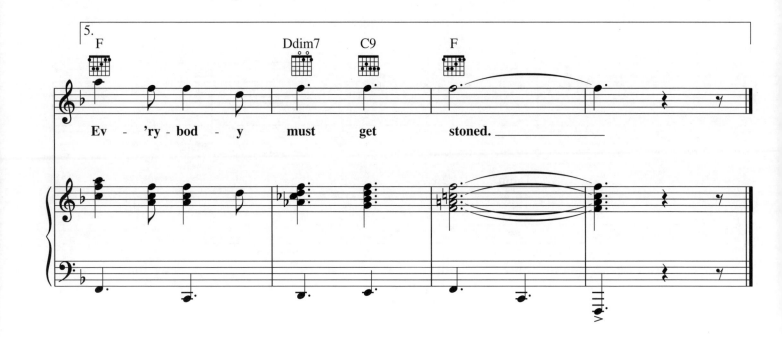

Additional Lyrics

2. Well, they'll stone ya when you're walkin' 'long the street.
   They'll stone ya when you're tryin' to keep your seat.
   They'll stone ya when you're walkin' on the floor.
   They'll stone ya when you're walkin' to the door.
   But I would not feel so all alone,
   Everybody must get stoned.

3. They'll stone ya when you're at the breakfast table.
   They'll stone ya when you are young and able.
   They'll stone ya when you're tryin' to make a buck.
   They'll stone ya and then they'll say, "Good luck."
   Tell ya what, I would not feel so all alone,
   Everybody must get stoned.

4. Well, they'll stone you and say that it's the end.
   Then they'll stone you and then they'll come back again.
   They'll stone you when you're riding in your car.
   They'll stone you when you're playing your guitar.
   Yes, but I would not feel so all alone,
   Everybody must get stoned.

5. Well, they'll stone you when you walk all alone.
   They'll stone you when you are walking home.
   They'll stone you and then say you are brave.
   They'll stone you when you are set down in your grave.
   But I would not feel so all alone,
   Everybody must get stoned.

Rikki Don't Lose That Number

Words and Music by
Walter Becker and Donald Fagen

I guess you kind of scared your-self, you turn _____ and run. _____
We could stay in side and play games I _____ don't know. _____

But if you have a change of heart, _____
And you could have a change of heart. _____

Rik - ki, don't lose that num - ber; you don't wan - na

call no - bod - y else. _____

Send it off in a

let-ter to your - self.

Rik-ki, don't lose that num - ber; it's the on-ly one you own.

You might use it if you feel bet - ter

when you get _____ home.

Rock & Roll - Part II
(The Hey Song)

Words and Music by
Mike Leander and Gary Glitter

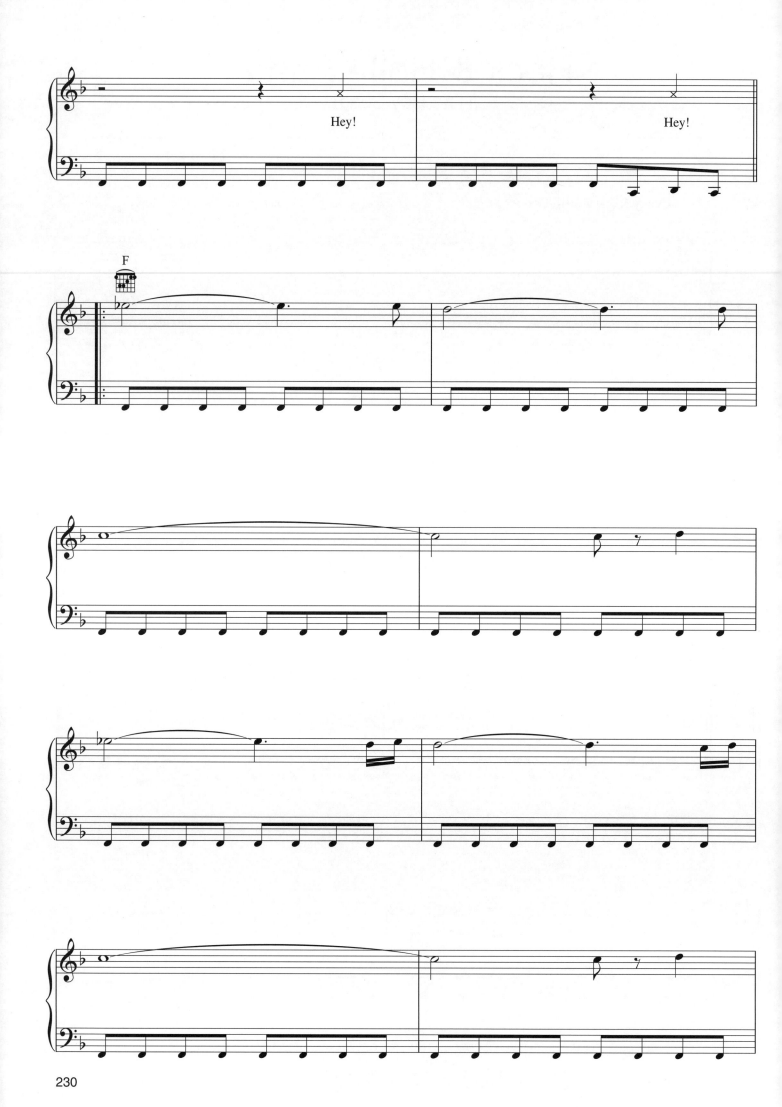

230

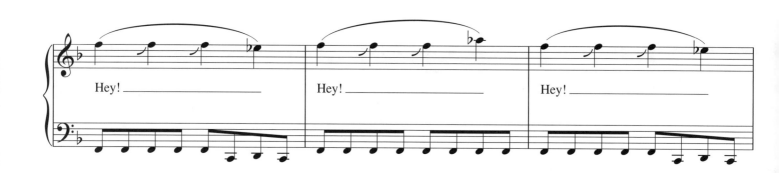

Rock'n Me

Words and Music by
Steve Miller

Moderate Rock beat

Well, I've been look-in' real hard and I'm
Don't get sus - pi - cious, now

try'n' to find a job, but it just keeps get - tin' tough-er ev - 'ry day. But I got ___
don't be sus - pi - cious, babe, you know you are a friend of mine. ___ And you know ___

___ to do my part 'cause I know in my heart I got to please my sweet ba - by, yeah. ___
___ that it's true that all the things that I do ___ are gon - na come back to you in your sweet time. ___

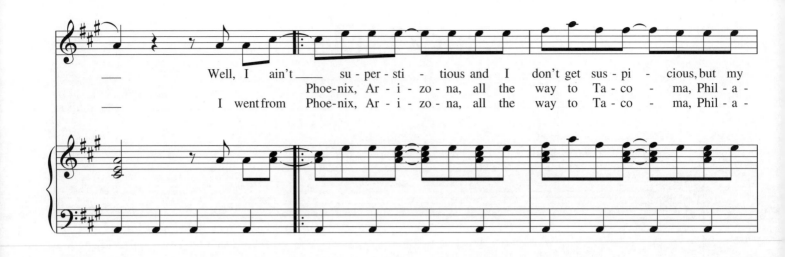

Well, I ain't ___ su - per - sti - tious and I don't get sus - pi - cious, but my

Phoe-nix, Ar - i - zo - na, all the way to Ta - co - ma, Phil - a -

I went from Phoe-nix, Ar - i - zo - na, all the way to Ta - co - ma, Phil - a -

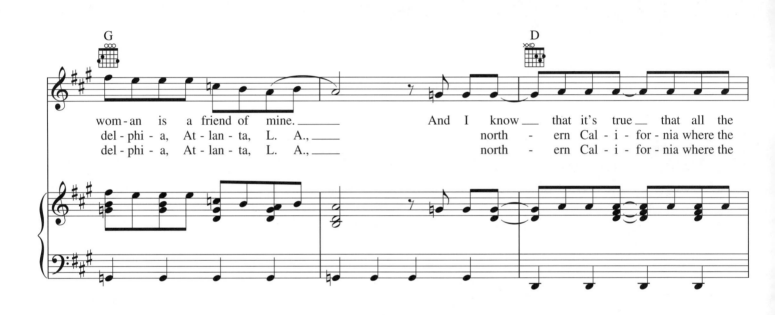

G   D

wom - an is a friend of mine. ___ And I know ___ that it's true ___ that all the

del - phi - a, At - lan - ta, L. A., ___ north - ern Cal - i - for - nia where the

del - phi - a, At - lan - ta, L. A., ___ north - ern Cal - i - for - nia where the

A   To Coda ⊕

things that I do ___ will come back ___ to me in my sweet time. ___ So keep on }

girls are warm ___ so I could be with my sweet ba - by, yeah. ___ Keep on a -

girls are warm ___ so I could hear my sweet, mm, ba - by say: ___ Keep on a -

Rosanna

Words and Music by
David Paich

Nev - er thought that a girl like you_ could ev - er care for me,_
I did - n't know that a girl like you_ could make me feel so sad,_

Ro - san - na._
Ro - san - na._

All I wan - na do in the mid - dle of the eve - ning is
All I wan - na tell you is now you'll nev - er, ev - er have to

hold you tight,_ Ro - san - na, Ro - san - na.
com - pro - mise,_ Ro - san - na, Ro - san - na.

have to say:__

Meet you all the way,

meet you all the way,

Ro - san - na,_____ yeah.__ Meet you

240

Show Me the Way

Words and Music by
Peter Frampton

I won-der how you're feel-ing. There's
I can see no rea-son. You're

ring - ing   in ___ my   ears, ___   and   no   one   to   re - late ___
liv - ing   on ___ your   nerves, ___   when   some - one   drops   a   cup, ___

___ to ___   'cept ___   the   sea. ___
___ and   I ___   sub - merge. ___   I'm

Who   can   I ___   be - lieve in? ___   I'm   kneel - ing   on ___   the   floor. ___
swim - ming   in ___   a   cir - cle; ___   I   feel   I'm   go - ing   down. ___

___   There   has   to   be ___   a   force;   who   do ___
___   There   has   to   be ___   a   fool   to   play ___

I won-der if ___ I'm dream-ing.

___ I feel so un - a - shamed; ___ I

can't be-lieve ___ this is hap - pen-ing ___ to me. ___

Sister Christian

Words and Music by
Kelly Keagy

Slow Ride

Words and Music by
Lonesome Dave Peverett

Slow ride, ____ take it eas - y. ____

Slow ride, ____ take it eas - y. ____

I'm in the mood, ____ the rhy-thm is right. ____

Repeat and Fade

254

Small Town

Words and Music by
John Mellencamp

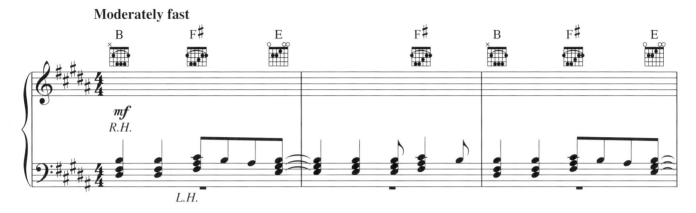

Well, I was born in a small __ town,
Ed - u - cat - ed in __ a small __ town,

and I live in a small __ town;
taught the fear of Je - sus in a small town;

prob -'ly die in a small __
used to day dream in that

Got noth-ing a-gainst a big town, still hay-seed e-nough to say "Look who's in the big town." But my bed is in a small town; oh, and that's good e-nough for me.

Something in the Air

Words and Music by
John Keen

Space Oddity

Words and Music by
David Bowie

Moderately slow

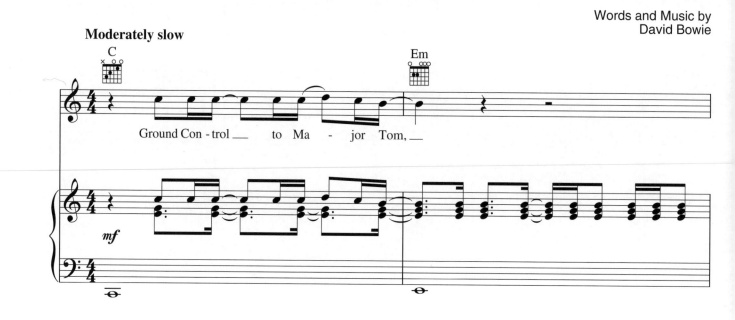

Ground Con-trol __ to Ma - jor Tom, __

Ground Con-trol __ to Ma - jor Tom: __

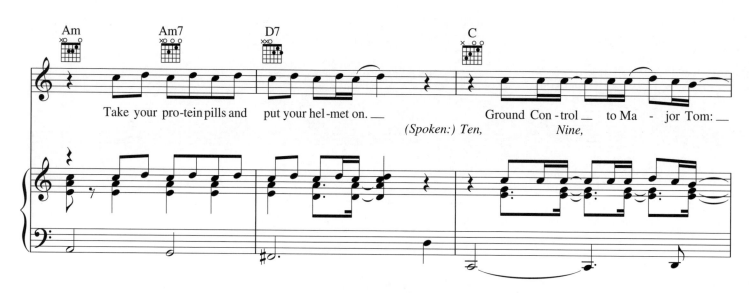

Take your pro-tein pills and put your hel-met on. __   Ground Con-trol __ to Ma - jor Tom: __

(Spoken:) Ten,   *Nine,*

And the pa- pers want to know _ whose shirts you wear. _
and I'm float- ing in a most _ pe- cu - li- ar way. _

Now it's time to leave the cap- sule if you dare. _____
And the stars _ look ver- y dif- fer- ent to - day. _____

For

here am I sit- ting in a tin can _ far _____ a- bove _ the world. _
Here am I float- ing 'round my tin can _ far _____ a- bove _ the moon. _

Plan- et Earth _ is blue and there's noth- ing I can

266

Still Crazy after All These Years

Words and Music by
Paul Simon

why should I?_____ It's all _____ gon-na

fade.

Now I sit by my win-dow and I

watch the cars; I fear I'll do some dam-age one fine

Tangled Up in Blue

Words and Music by
Bob Dylan

Tan - gled up in blue. __
tan - gled up in blue. __

4. She was working in a topless place
   And I stopped in for a beer.
   I just kept looking at the side of her face
   In the spotlight so clear.
   And later on when the crowd thinned out
   I was just about to do the same.
   She was standing there in back of my chair,
   Said to me, "Don't I know your name?"
   I muttered something underneath my breath.
   She studied the lines on my face.
   I must admit I felt a little uneasy
   When she bent down to tie the laces of my shoe,
   Tangled up in blue.

5. She lit a burner on the stove
   And offered me a pipe.
   "I thought you'd never say hello," she said.
   "You look like the silent type."
   Then she opened up a book of poems
   And handed it to me,
   Written by an Italian poet
   From the thirteenth century.
   And every one of them words rang true
   And glowed like burning coal,
   Pourin' off of every page
   Like it was written in my soul,
   From me to you,
   Tangled up in blue.

6. I lived with them on Montague Street
   In a basement down the stairs.
   There was music in the cafes at night
   And revolution in the air.
   Then he started in the dealing in slaves
   And something inside of him died.
   She had to sell everything she owned
   And froze up inside.
   And when finally the bottom finally fell out
   I became withdrawn.
   The only thing I knew how to do
   Was to keep on keeping on,
   Like a bird that flew
   Tangled up in blue.

7. So now I'm going back again.
   I got to get to her somehow.
   All the people we used to know,
   They're an illusion to me now.
   Some are mathematicians,
   Some are carpenter's wives.
   Don't know how it all got started,
   I don't know what they do with their lives.
   But me, I'm still on the road
   Headin' for another joint.
   We always did feel the same,
   We just saw it from a different point of view,
   Tangled up in blue.

Thick As a Brick

Words and Music by
Ian Anderson

And the

And the love that I feel____

is so far__ a - way.____

I'm a bad dream that I just had _____ to - day. _____

And you shake_ your head and said it's a shame.

Spin me back down_ the years _____ and_ the days _____

Tiny Dancer

Words and Music by
Elton John and Bernie Taupin

And now____ she's in____ me,__ al - ways_ with____ me,__
Look - ing on, _____ she sings the __ songs. _____

ti - ny danc - er____ in my____ hand. _____
The word she __ knows, the tune she____ hums. _____

1.

2.

But oh how it feels_ so real __

way.

Lay me down _ in sheets _ of lin -

en.

You had a bus - y day _ to - day. _

*D.S. al Coda

*On Verse repeat, take 2nd ending;
on Chorus repeat, take both endings.

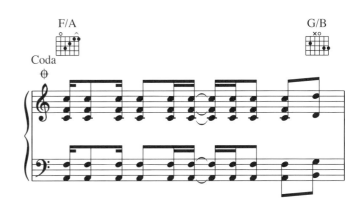

Coda

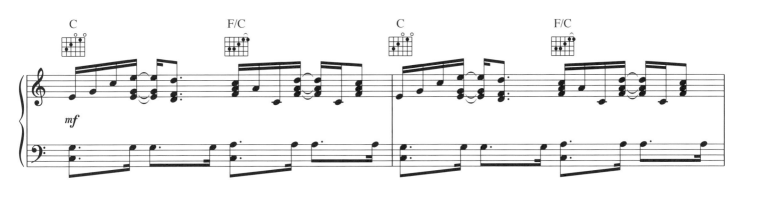

rit.

287

Walk Away Renee

Words and Music by
Mike Brown, Tony Sansone
and Bob Calilli

289

290

We Are the Champions

Words and Music by
Freddie Mercury

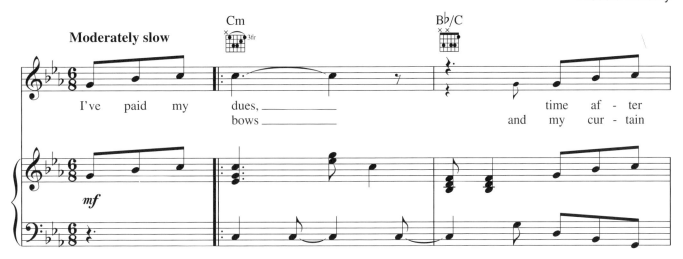

I've paid my dues, time af-ter
bows and my cur-tain

time. I've done my sen-tence
calls. You brought me fame and for-tune and ev-'ry-thing that

but com-mit-ted no crime.
goes with it, I thank you all.

We _____ are the cham - pions, ____ my friend. _____
(D.S.) world. _____

And we'll _____ keep on fight - ing _____ till the

end. _____ We are the

cham - pions. We are the cham - pions.

No time for los - ers, 'cause we are the cham - pions

of the world.

I've tak - en my

of the

cham - pions.

A Whiter Shade of Pale

Words and Music by
Keith Reid, Gary Brooker
and Matthew Fisher

We skipped the light fan - dan - go,
She said, "I'm home on shore leave,"
She said, "There is no rea - son,

turned cart - wheels __ 'cross the floor;
though in truth we __ were at sea. __
and the truth is __ plain to see." __

I was feel - ing kind of sea - sick,
So I took her by the look - ing glass
But I wan - dered through my play - ing cards

the crowd called __ out __ for more.
and forced her __ to __ a - gree,
and would not __ let __ her be

The room was hum - ming hard - er
say - ing, "You must be the mer - maid
one of six - teen ves - tal vir - gins

296

as the mill - er told his tale, ____

that her face at first just ghost - ly ____ turned a

whit - er ____ shade of pale. ____

pale. ____

pale. ____

More Great Piano/Vocal Books

FROM CHERRY LANE

For a complete listing of Cherry Lane titles available,
including contents listings, please visit our web site at
www.cherrylane.com

  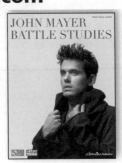 

More Big-Note & Easy Piano Books

For a complete listing of Cherry Lane titles available, including contents listings, please visit our web site at www.cherrylane.

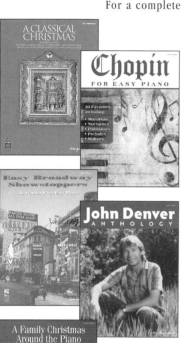

CHOPIN FOR EASY PIANO

This special easy piano version features the composer's intricate melodies, harmonies and rhythms newly arranged so that virtually all pianists can experience the thrill of playing Chopin at the piano! Includes 20 favorites mazurkas, nocturnes, polonaises, preludes and waltzes.
_____02501483 Easy Piano...............$7.99

CLASSICAL CHRISTMAS

Easy solo arrangements of 30 wonderful holiday songs: Ave Maria • Dance of the Sugar Plum Fairy • Evening Prayer • Gesu Bambino • Hallelujah! • He Shall Feed His Flock • March of the Toys • O Come, All Ye Faithful • O Holy Night • Pastoral Symphony • Sheep May Safely Graze • Sinfonia • Waltz of the Flowers • and more.
_____02500112 Easy Piano Solo.......$9.95

BEST OF JOHN DENVER

A collection of 18 Denver classics, including: Leaving on a Jet Plane • Take Me Home, Country Roads • Rocky Mountain High • Follow Me • and more.
_____02505512 Easy Piano...............$9.95

JOHN DENVER ANTHOLOGY

Easy arrangements of 34 of the finest from this beloved artist. Includes: Annie's Song • Fly Away • Follow Me • Grandma's Feather Bed • Leaving on a Jet Plane • Perhaps Love • Rocky Mountain High • Sunshine on My Shoulders • Take Me Home, Country Roads • Thank God I'm a Country Boy • and many more.
_____02501366 Easy Piano.............$19.99

EASY BROADWAY SHOWSTOPPERS

Easy piano arrangements of 16 traditional and new Broadway standards, including: "Impossible Dream" from _Man of La Mancha_ • "Unusual Way" from _Nine_ • "This Is the Moment" from _Jekyll & Hyde_ • many more.
_____02505517 Easy Piano.............$12.95

A FAMILY CHRISTMAS AROUND THE PIANO

25 songs for hours of family fun, including: Away in a Manger • Deck the Hall • The First Noel • God Rest Ye Merry, Gentlemen • Hark! the Herald Angels Sing • Jingle Bells • Jolly Old St. Nicholas • Joy to the World • O Little Town of Bethlehem • Silent Night, Holy Night • The Twelve Days of Christmas • and more.
_____02500398 Easy Piano...............$8.99

FAVORITE CELTIC SONGS FOR EASY PIANO

Easy arrangements of 40 Celtic classics, including: The Ash Grove • The Bluebells of Scotland • A Bunch of Thyme • Danny Boy • Finnegan's Wake • I'll Tell Me Ma • Loch Lomond • My Wild Irish Rose • The Rose of Tralee • and more!
_____02501306 Easy Piano.............$12.99

FAVORITE POP BALLADS

This new collection features 35 beloved ballads, including: Breathe (2 AM) • Faithfully • Leaving on a Jet Plane • Open Arms • Ordinary People • Summer Breeze • These Eyes • Truly • You've Got a Friend • and more.
_____02501005 Easy Piano.............$15.99

HOLY CHRISTMAS CAROLS COLORING BOOK

A terrific songbook with 7 sacred carols and lots of coloring pages for the young pianist. Songs include: Angels We Have Heard on High • The First Noel • Hark! The Herald Angels Sing • It Came upon a Midnight Clear • O Come All Ye Faithful • O Little Town of Bethlehem • Silent Night.
_____02500277 Five-Finger Piano $6.95

JEKYLL & HYDE – VOCAL SELECTIONS

Ten songs from the Wildhorn/Bricusse Broadway smash, arranged for big-note: In His Eyes • It's a Dangerous Game • Lost in the Darkness • A New Life • No One Knows Who I Am • Once Upon a Dream • Someone Like You • Sympathy, Tenderness • Take Me as I Am • This Is the Moment.
_____02500023 Big-Note Piano $9.95

JACK JOHNSON ANTHOLOGY

Easy arrangements of 27 of the best from this Hawaiian singer/songwriter, including: Better Together • Breakdown • Flake • Fortunate Fool • Good People • Sitting, Waiting, Wishing • Taylor • and more.
_____02501313 Easy Piano.............$19.99

JUST FOR KIDS – _NOT!_ CHRISTMAS SONGS

This unique collection of 14 Christmas favorites is fun for the whole family! Kids can play the full-sounding big-note solos alone, or with their parents (or teachers) playing accompaniment for the thrill of four-hand piano! Includes: Deck the Halls • Jingle Bells • Silent Night • What Child Is This? • and more.
_____02505510 Big-Note Piano $8.95

JUST FOR KIDS – _NOT!_ CLASSICS

Features big-note arrangements of classical masterpieces, plus optional accompaniment for adults. Songs: Air on the G String • Dance of the Sugar Plum Fairy • Für Elise • Jesu, Joy of Man's Desiring • Ode to Joy • Pomp and Circumstance • The Sorcerer's Apprentice • William Tell Overture • and more!
_____02505513 Classics $7.95
_____02500301 More Classics..........$8.95

JUST FOR KIDS – _NOT!_ FUN SONGS

Fun favorites for kids everywhere in big-note arrangements for piano, including: Bingo • Eensy Weensy Spider • Farmer in the Dell • Jingle Bells • London Bridge • Pop Goes the Weasel • Puff the Magic Dragon • Skip to My Lou • Twinkle, Twinkle Little Star • and more!
_____02505523 Fun Songs $7.95

JUST FOR KIDS – _NOT!_ TV THEMES & MOVIE SONGS

Entice the kids to the piano with this delightful collection of songs and themes from movies and TV. These big-note arrangements include themes from The Brady Bunch and The Addams Family, as well as Do-Re-Mi (The Sound of Music), theme from Beetlejuice (Day-O) and Puff the Magic Dragon. Each song includes an accompaniment part for teacher or adult so that the kids can experience the joy of four-hand playing as well! Plus performance tips.
_____02505507 TV Themes & Movie Songs......................$9.95
_____02500304 More TV Themes & Movie Songs......................$9.95

MERRY CHRISTMAS, EVERYONE

Over 20 contemporary and classic all-time holiday favorites arranged for big-note piano or easy piano. Includes: Away in a Manger • Christmas Like a Lullaby • The First Noel • Joy to the World • The Marvelous Toy • and more.
_____02505600 Big-Note Piano $9.95

POKEMON 2 B.A. MASTER

This great songbook features easy piano arrangements of 13 tunes from the hit TV series: 2.B.A. Master • Double Trouble (Team Rocket) • Everything Changes • Misty's Song • My Best Friends • Pokémon (Dance Mix) • Pokémon Theme • PokéRAP • The Time Has Come (Pikachu's Goodbye) • Together, Forever • Viridian City • What Kind of Pokémon Are You? • You Can Do It (If You Really Try). Includes a full-color, 8-page pull-out section featuring characters and scenes from this super hot show.
_____02500145 Easy Piano.............$12.95

POP/ROCK LOVE SONGS

Easy arrangements of 18 romatic favorites, including: Always • Bed of Roses • Butterfly Kisses • Follow Me • From This Moment On • Hard Habit to Break • Leaving on a Jet Plane • When You Say Nothing at All • more.
_____02500151 Easy Piano.............$10.95

POPULAR CHRISTMAS CAROLS COLORING BOOK

Kids are sure to love this fun holiday songbook! It features five-finger piano arrangements of seven Christmas classics, complete with coloring pages throughout! Songs include: Deck the Hall • Good King Wenceslas • Jingle Bells • Jolly Old St. Nicholas • O Christmas Tree • Up on the Housetop • We Wish You a Merry Christmas.
_____02500276 Five-Finger Piano $6.95

PUFF THE MAGIC DRAGON & 54 OTHER ALL-TIME CHILDREN'S FAVORITESONGS

55 timeless songs enjoyed by generations of kids, and sure to be favorites for years to come. Songs include: A-Tisket A-Tasket • Alouette • Eensy Weensy Spider • The Farmer in the Dell • I've Been Working on the Railroad • If You're Happy and You Know It • Joy to the World • Michael Finnegan • Oh Where, Oh Where Has My Little Dog Gone • Silent Night • Skip to My Lou • This Old Man • and many more.
_____02500017 Big-Note Piano $12.95

See your local music dealer or contact:

EXCLUSIVELY DISTRIBUTED BY
7777 W. BLUEMOUND RD. P.O. BOX 13819 MILWAUKEE, WI 53213

Prices, contents, and availability subject to change without notice.

0811

great songs series

This legendary series has delighted players and performers for generations.

Great Songs of the Fifties

Features rock, pop, country, Broadway and movie tunes, including: All Shook Up • At the Hop • Blue Suede Shoes • Dream Lover • Fly Me to the Moon • Kansas City • Love Me Tender • Misty • Peggy Sue • Rock Around the Clock • Sea of Love • Sixteen Tons • Take the "A" Train • Wonderful! Wonderful! • and more. Includes an introduction by award-winning journalist Bruce Pollock.
02500323 P/V/G.......................................$16.95

Great Songs of the Sixties, Vol. 1 – Revised

The updated version of this classic book includes 80 faves from the 1960s: Angel of the Morning • Bridge over Troubled Water • Cabaret • Different Drum • Do You Believe in Magic • Eve of Destruction • Monday, Monday • Spinning Wheel • Walk on By • and more.
02509902 P/V/G.......................................$19.95

Great Songs of the Sixties, Vol. 2 – Revised

61 more '60s hits: California Dreamin' • Crying • For Once in My Life • Honey • Little Green Apples • MacArthur Park • Me and Bobby McGee • Nowhere Man • Piece of My Heart • Sugar, Sugar • You Made Me So Very Happy • and more.
02509904 P/V/G.......................................$19.95

Great Songs of the Seventies, Vol. 1 – Revised

This super collection of 70 big hits from the '70s includes: After the Love Has Gone • Afternoon Delight • Annie's Song • Band on the Run • Cold as Ice • FM • Imagine • It's Too Late • Layla • Let It Be • Maggie May • Piano Man • Shelter from the Storm • Superstar • Sweet Baby James • Time in a Bottle • The Way We Were • and more.
02509917 P/V/G.......................................$19.95

Great Songs of the Eighties – Revised

This edition features 50 songs in rock, pop & country styles, plus hits from Broadway and the movies! Songs: Almost Paradise • Angel of the Morning • Do You Really Want to Hurt Me • Endless Love • Flashdance...What a Feeling • Guilty • Hungry Eyes • (Just Like) Starting Over • Let Love Rule • Missing You • Patience • Through the Years • Time After Time • Total Eclipse of the Heart • and more.
02502125 P/V/G.......................................$18.95

Great Songs of the Nineties

Includes: Achy Breaky Heart • Beautiful in My Eyes • Believe • Black Hole Sun • Black Velvet • Blaze of Glory • Building a Mystery • Crash into Me • Fields of Gold • From a Distance • Glycerine • Here and Now • Hold My Hand • I'll Make Love to You • Ironic • Linger • My Heart Will Go On • Waterfalls • Wonderwall • and more.
02500040 P/V/G.......................................$16.95

Great Songs of 2000-2009

Over 50 of the decade's biggest hits, including: Accidentally in Love • Breathe (2 AM) • Daughters • Hanging by a Moment • The Middle • The Remedy (I Won't Worry) • Smooth • A Thousand Miles • and more.
02500922 P/V/G.......................................$24.99

Great Songs of Broadway – Revised Edition

This updated edition is loaded with 54 hits: And All That Jazz • Be Italian • Comedy Tonight • Consider Yourself • Dulcinea • Edelweiss • Friendship • Getting to Know You • Hopelessly Devoted to You • If I Loved You • The Impossible Dream • Mame • On My Own • On the Street Where You Live • People • Try to Remember • Unusual Way • When You're Good to Mama • Where Is Love? • and more.
02501545 P/V/G.......................................$19.99

Great Songs for Children

90 wonderful, singable favorites kids love: Baa Baa Black Sheep • Bingo • The Candy Man • Do-Re-Mi • Eensy Weensy Spider • The Hokey Pokey • Linus and Lucy • Sing • This Old Man • Yellow Submarine • and more, with a touching foreword by Grammy-winning singer/songwriter Tom Chapin.
02501348 P/V/G.......................................$19.99

Prices, contents, and availability subject to change without notice.

Great Songs of Christmas

59 yuletide favorites in piano/vocal/guitar format, including: Breath of Heaven (Mary's Song) • Christmas Time Is Here • Frosty the Snow Man • I'll Be Home for Christmas • Jingle-Bell Rock • Nuttin' for Christmas • O Little Town of Bethlehem • Silver Bells • The Twelve Days of Christmas • What Child Is This? • and many more.
02501543 P/V/G.......................................$17.99

Great Songs of Country Music

This volume features 58 country gems, including: Abilene • Afternoon Delight • Amazed • Annie's Song • Blue Crazy • Elvira • Fly Away • For the Good Times • Friends in Low Places • The Gambler • Hey, Good Lookin' • I Hope You Dance • Thank God I'm a Country Boy • This Kiss • Your Cheatin' Heart • and more.
02500503 P/V/G.......................................$19.95

Great Songs of Folk Music

Nearly 50 of the most popular folk songs of our time, including: Blowin' in the Wind • The House of the Rising Sun • Puff the Magic Dragon • This Land Is Your Land • Time in a Bottle • The Times They Are A-Changin' • The Unicorn • Where Have All the Flowers Gone? • and more.
02500997 P/V/G.......................................$19.95

Great Songs from The Great American Songbook

52 American classics, including: Ain't That a Kick in the Head • As Time Goes By • Come Fly with Me •Georgia on My Mind • I Get a Kick Out of You • I've Got You Under My Skin • The Lady Is a Tramp • Love and Marriage • Mack the Knife • Misty • Over the Rainbow • People • Take the "A" Train • Thanks for the Memory • and more.
02500760 P/V/G.......................................$16.95

Great Songs of the Movies

Nearly 60 of the best songs popularized in the movies, including: Accidentally in Love • Alfie • Almost Paradise • The Rainbow Connection • Somewhere in My Memory • Take My Breath Away (Love Theme) • Three Coins in the Fountain • (I've Had) the Time of My Life • Up Where We Belong • The Way We Were • and more.
02500967 P/V/G.......................................$19.95

Great Songs of the Pop Era

Over 50 hits from the pop era, including: Every Breath You Take • I'm Every Woman • Just the Two of Us • Leaving on a Jet Plane • My Cherie Amour • Raindrops Keep Fallin' on My Head • Time After Time • (I've Had) the Time of My Life • What a Wonderful World • and more.
02500043 Easy Piano.......................................$16.95

Great Songs for Weddings

A beautiful collection of 59 pop standards perfect for wedding ceremonies and receptions, including: Always and Forever • Amazed • Beautiful in My Eyes • Can You Feel the Love Tonight • Endless Love • Love of a Lifetime • Open Arms • Unforgettable • When I Fall in Love • The Wind Beneath My Wings • and more.
02501006 P/V/G.......................................$19.95

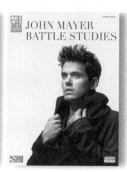

Great DVD selections from CHERRY LANE